A Book of
PERSONAL PRAYER

A Book of
PERSONAL PRAYER

René O. Bideaux

COMPILER

UPPER ROOM BOOKS
Nashville

A BOOK OF PERSONAL PRAYER
© 1997 by The Upper Room
All rights reserved.

No part of this book may be used or reproduced in any manner whatsoever without permission except in the case of brief quotations embodied in critical articles or reviews. For information write: Upper Room books, P.O. Box 189, Nashville, TN 37202-0189.

Upper Room Web Site: http://www.upperroom.org

Cover design: Bruce Gore

First printing: May 1997 (10)

Page 147 constitutes an extension of this copyright page.

Library of Congress Cataloging-in-Publication
A book of personal prayer / René O. Bideaux, compiler.
      p.   cm.
   Includes bibliographical references.
   ISBN 0-8358-0812-2 (hardback)
   1. Prayers. I. Bideaux, René O.
BV245.B588 1997
242'.8—dc21   97-17257
                                                   CIP

Printed in the United States of America on acid-free paper

Contents

INTRODUCTION 7
RELATING TO GOD 11
Through awe, gratitude, and praise .. 12
Through humility and contrition ... 23
Through God's faithfulness
   and guidance 33

RESPONDING TO CHRIST 41
Through confession, forgiveness,
   and surrender 42
Through suffering and healing 56
Through daily life and witnessing ... 76

RIPENING IN THE SPIRIT 91
Through Word and prayer 92
Through the love, joy, and peace
   of God 104

Through truth, discernment, and
  perseverance 120
Through reconciliation, justice, and unity
  in Christ 126

ACKNOWLEDGMENTS. 146

ABOUT THE COMPILER 159

Introduction

AN EARLY CHRISTIAN MASTER Brother Charles of Jesus prayed, "I abandon myself into your hands; do with me what you will." What God "wills" is to pursue us, to convince us, and to sanctify us. To pray in this spirit means we invite God to initiate and form the petition: "Not my will, but thy will be done." Such complete self-abandonment allows God's grace to control our relationships, direct our responses, and secure a maturing faith.

How do we as twenty-first century Christians go about this? In a world that advocates independence, self-control, and self-reliance, how do we begin the self-abandonment so that God might form us into the likeness of Jesus Christ?

Introduction

Our early Christian mothers and fathers practiced living with a prayer, with one prayer that touched their being in a special way. For days, for weeks, for months, they prayed that one prayer again and again. In the beginning they read the prayer, and the prayer was in their minds. They focused on the words and the meanings behind those words.

As time passed in praying this same prayer, our mothers and fathers in the faith began to know the words so well that they no longer needed to read the prayer; the prayer was on their lips. While the prayer was on their lips, they began to focus on ways the prayer reflected the nature of God revealed in the Hebrew Scriptures and then on the ways the prayer reflected the life and teachings of Jesus. They were able to speak the prayer to others as a prayer of

Introduction

their own. As they continued to pray, the prayer moved to their hearts. The prayer became a deep desire of their being; the prayer became an expression of their longing to be one with God and the risen Christ.

And eventually, they found the ability and the courage to act on the prayer, to go into the world to live as the prayer directed. That is to say, finally, they became the embodiment of that prayer with which they had lived for so long. The prayer migrated from the mind, to the lips, to the heart. The persons praying the prayer were transformed in some small way into the likeness of Jesus Christ. They had abandoned their self-will to God's initiative. This classic pattern is a timely model for contemporary Christians.

This pocket book of personal prayers offers a limited collection of prayers that reveals the same spirit of abandonment to God's initiative. The prayers represent a diversity of spiritual journeys from scripture and throughout the church's history. Language adaptations have made the prayers more accessible. May the movement of the prayers from head to lips to heart enrich and transform your life. As Martin Luther reflected,

> *It is well to let prayer be the first employment in the early morning and the last in the evening. Avoid diligently those false and deceptive thoughts which say, "wait a little. I will pray an hour hence; I must first perform this or that." For with such thoughts people quit prayer for business, which lays hold of and entangles them so that they come not to pray the whole day long.*

~ René O. Bideaux

Relating to God

Relating to God

Our Father in heaven,
hallowed be your name,
your kingdom come,
your will be done, on earth
as in heaven.
Give us today our daily bread.
Forgive us our sins
as we forgive those who sin
against us.
Save us from the time of trial
and deliver us from evil.
For the kingdom, the power, and the
glory are yours now and for ever.
Amen.

~ *Ecumenical Text*

Through awe, gratitude, and praise

Gracious God, I put myself before you in this moment with waiting heart, expectant desire. Open my eyes that I may see your promise fulfilled; open my ears that I may hear your word whispered to my deepest being. Amen.

~ *Norman Shawchuck, twentieth century*

Bless the Lord, O my soul;
and all that is within me,
bless his holy name!
Bless the Lord, O my soul,
and forget not all his benefits.

~ *Psalm 103:1-2*, RSV

ou are holy, Lord, the only God and your deeds are wonderful.
You are strong, you are great.
You are the most High, you are almighty.
You, holy Father, are King of heaven and earth.
You are Three and One, Lord God, all good.
You are good, all good, supreme good, Lord God, living and true.
You are love, you are wisdom.
You are humility, you are endurance.
You are rest, you are peace.
You are joy and gladness,
 you are justice and moderation.
You are beauty, you are gentleness.
You are our protector, you are our guardian and defender.

Through awe, gratitude, and praise

You are courage, you are our haven
and our hope.
You are our faith, our great
consolation.
You are our eternal life, great and
wonderful Lord,
God almighty, merciful Saviour.

~ *Francis of Assisi, 1181–1226*

O Lord, our Sovereign,
how majestic is your name
in all the earth!

~ *Psalm 8:1*

Relating to God

O God, we thank you for this earth, our home; for the wide sky and the blessed sun, for the salt sea and the running water, for the everlasting hills and the never-resting winds, for trees and the common grass underfoot. We thank you for our senses by which we hear the songs of birds, and see the splendour of the summer fields, and taste of the autumn fruits, and rejoice in the feel of the snow, and smell the breath of the spring. Grant us a heart wide open to all this beauty; and save our souls from being so blind that we pass unseeing when even the common thornbush is aflame with your glory, O God our creator, who lives and reigns for ever and ever.

~ *Walter Rauschenbusch, 1861–1918*

Through awe, gratitude, and praise

I will praise you, O Lord, with all my heart;
  I will tell of all your wonders.
I will be glad and rejoice in you;
  I will sing praise to your name, O Most High.

~ *Psalm 9:1-2, NIV*

Dear God, we thank you for food we eat, the clothes we wear, and the roof that we live under. We pray for the people that have no home and that they will find a home. And we pray for all the people in the hospital that they get well.

~ *Erin, age 8*

Relating to God

O Great Spirit, whose breath gives life to the world, and whose voice is heard in the soft breeze: We need your strength and wisdom.

Cause us to walk in beauty. Give us eyes ever to behold the red and purple sunset. Make us wise so that we may understand what you have taught us.

Help us learn the lessons you have hidden in every leaf and rock. Make us always ready to come to you with clean hands and steady eyes, so when life fades, like the fading sunset, our spirits may come to you without shame.

~ *Traditional Native American Prayer*

Through awe, gratitude, and praise

You are compassion and grace, almighty God. I join your creatures everywhere in blessing your name, holy and loving One. Glory be to the Father, Son, and Holy Spirit, world without end. Amen.

~ *Elise S. Eslinger, twentieth century*

I call upon you, O Lord; come quickly to me;
give ear to my voice when I call to you.
Let my prayer be counted as incense before you,
and the lifting up of my hands as an evening sacrifice.

~ *Psalm 141:1-2*

Relating to God

O Lord, Creator,
Ruler of the world, Father,
I thank, thank, thank you
that you have brought me through.
How strong the pain was—
but you were stronger.
How deep the fall was—
but you were even deeper.
How dark was the night—
but you were the noonday sun in it.
You are our father,
our mother,
our brother and our friend.
Your grace has no end,
and your light no snuffer.

~ *An African Prayer*

Through awe, gratitude, and praise

Thanks be to you, Lord Jesus Christ, for all the benefits which you have won for us, for all the pains and insults which you have borne for us. O most merciful Redeemer, Friend and Brother, may we know you more clearly, love you more dearly, and follow you more nearly day by day.

~ *Richard of Chichester, 1197–1253*

Relating to God

Dear God, the source and sustainer of my being: You have richly endowed me with all things for my sustenance. With praise on my lips and thanksgiving in my heart, I bow before you this day in blessed adoration. My spirit soars above the everydayness of worry and anxiety because I believe in your promise to always be with me in joy or in sorrow, and even when the pain of life is unrelieved. With gratitude I give this day into your hands, asking you to guide and direct my thoughts, feelings, and actions to the end that they may glorify you in deeds of love and faithful service. In Jesus' name I pray. Amen!

~ *Edward G. Carroll, Sr., twentieth century*

Through humility and con

Ever-watchful God knows the heart and secret desires of all persons, search my heart, I pray. See if there be any harm in me, and lead me in your way—forever. I pray in the name of your own gentle Spirit. Amen.

~ *Norman Shawchuck, twentieth century*

s a deer longs for flowing streams,
so my soul longs for you, O God.
My soul thirsts for God,
for the living God.

~ *Psalm 42:1-2*

Relating to God

Grant, O Lord, that I may look for nothing, claim nothing, and resent nothing; that I may go through all the scenes of life, not seeking my own glory, but looking wholly unto you and acting wholly for you.

~ *John Wesley, 1703–1791*

O Lord,
never suffer us to think
that we can stand by ourselves, and not need thee.

~ *John Donne, 1571–1631*

Through humility and contrition

O Lord, what are human beings
that you regard them,
or mortals that you think
of them?
They are like a breath; their days are
like a passing shadow.

~ *Psalm 144:3-4*

Thou hast made us for Thyself, and our hearts are restless till they rest in Thee.

~ *Augustine of Hippo, 354–430*

Relating to God

O God who calls my name,
There was a scar in my center where I pulled away from you.
Searching for my name,
I let others tell me who I was.
There was a wound in your center where I pulled away from you.
You did not let it heal,
　so that I would have a place to come back to.
Teach me to un-walk, un-stand; to rest in the circle of your arms.
Unknot this cord of self-reliance, and flow your life in mine.
Feed me near the heart of God.
Let each faltering step be toward you.
Let sleep come with your song.
And morning come with your light.

~ *Ray Buckley, twentieth century*

Through humility and contrition

Use me then, my Saviour, for whatever purpose, and in whatever way, you may require. Here is my poor heart, an empty vessel; fill it with your grace. Here is my sinful and troubled soul; quicken it and refresh it with your love. Take my heart for your abode; my mouth to spread abroad the glory of your name; my love and all my powers, for the advancement of your believing people; and never suffer the steadfastness and confidence of my faith to abate; so that at all times I may be enabled from the heart to say, "Jesus needs me, and I am his."

~ *Dwight L. Moody, 1837–1899*

O Jesus, you did not allow the rage of accusers to carry the day against the woman caught. So do not, I pray, allow my self-righteous fits to bring condemnation before compassion.

Ever drive me to examine myself before I speak, before I act in anger and rage. Great Lord, command me to drop the stones.

~ *Gerrit Scott Dawson, twentieth century*

Through humility and contrition

O Lord, you have searched me and known me.
    You know when I sit down and when I rise up;
    you discern my thoughts from far away.
You search out my path and my lying down,
    and are acquainted with all my ways.
Even before a word is on my tongue,
    O Lord, you know it completely.
You hem me in, behind and before,
    and lay your hand upon me.
Such knowledge is too wonderful for me;
    it is so high that I cannot attain it.

~ Psalm 139:1-6

Behold, Lord, an empty vessel that needs to be filled. My Lord, fill it. I am weak in the faith; strengthen me. I am cold in love; warm me and make me fervent, that my love may go out to my neighbour. I do not have a strong and firm faith; at times I doubt and am unable to trust you altogether. O Lord, help me. Strengthen my faith and trust in you. In you I have sealed the treasure of all I have. I am poor; you are rich and came to be merciful to the poor. I am a sinner; you are upright. With me, there is an abundance of sin; in you is the fullness of righteousness. Therefore I will remain with you, of whom I can receive, but to whom I may not give.

~ *Martin Luther, 1483–1546*

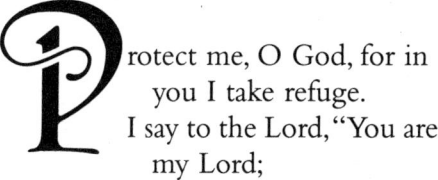

Protect me, O God, for in you I take refuge.
I say to the Lord, "You are my Lord;
I have no good apart from you."

. . . .

You show me the path of life.
In your presence there is fullness of joy;
in your right hand are pleasures forevermore.

~ *Psalm 16:1-2, 11*

Relating to God

I cry to you, O Lord;
I say, "You are my refuge,
my portion in the land of the
living."
Give heed to my cry,
for I am brought very low.

~ *Psalm 142:5-6*

Merciful God, through your love release me from all that binds me. Give me courage to step boldly forward in faith.

~ *George R. Graham, twentieth century*

Through God's faithfulness and guidance

Merciful God, were it not for your mercy, I would remain lost in sin and confusion. Thank you for your extravagant grace and your mercy without limit. In this hour hold me in love, even as a mother cradles her child. Amen.

~ *Norman Shawchuck, twentieth century*

I will sing of thy steadfast love, O Lord, for ever;
with my mouth I will proclaim thy faithfulness to all generations.

~ *Psalm 89:1, RSV*

Relating to God

ow long, O God, before the gift comes? This gift of faith for which I hunger and long.

You have heard my cries and prayers throughout the years. When you have tried to answer, I have resisted. Remain faithful to me, O God—do not forget me—do not give up on me.

I yet believe I can receive the gift—I yet believe you will bring the freedom for which I long. I know the day will come when my God will open the gates of my city and come in—and I will go out.

I know the day will come when my God brings to me the gift of faith for which I long. Praise the name of the Lord—my belief and your faithfulness sustain me.

~ *Steve Smith, twentieth century*

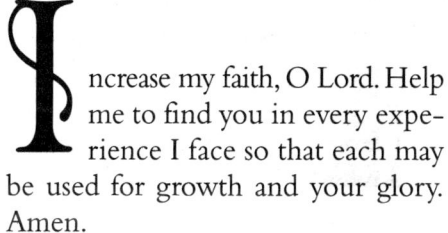

Increase my faith, O Lord. Help me to find you in every experience I face so that each may be used for growth and your glory. Amen.

~ *Joseph B. Bethea, twentieth century*

Relating to God

Eternal God,
Lord of all life,
I, your forgetful child, now remind myself of my final dependence upon your grace. So often in my prayers I use phrases like

"Remember me, O God,"

"Hear me now, O Lord,"

"Look with favor upon me."

How foolish such phrases are!

You remember me in the midst of my forgetting. You hear me when I make the tiniest squeak. You look with favor upon me when I cannot stand myself. But things are the other way round.

I am the one who needs to be reminded that you do not turn from me, I turn from you.

Through God's faithfulness and guidance

You do not forget me, I forget you.

You do not despise me even when I err and go astray, I despise myself. Old brown yesterdays haunt and trouble me. Old wounds ache, and old bruises give me pain.

Let me recall old promises. For you have said, "Ho, everyone who is thirsty, come to the waters, and he who has no money, come, buy and eat."

I am parched and dry, O Lord. I am hungry for affirmations in life. I come, tentatively, just hoping and not really believing. But I come. Amen.

~ *Kenneth G. Phifer, twentieth century*

Relating to God

God, you are my constant companion. Help me to see you in all things. May every object and event direct my attention to you.

May I find guideposts in my ordinary day which point to you. May common things of life become media of your presence. Give me:

> eyes to see,
> ears to hear,
> fingers to touch,
> smells and taste
> of your presence

May daily rounds of life present reminders of your presence, incitements to prayer for others, and openings for service. In the name of our incarnate Lord. Amen.

~ *Thomas A. Langford, twentieth century*

Through God's faithfulness and guidance

The Lord bless you and keep you;
the Lord make his face to shine upon you, and be gracious to you;
the Lord lift up his countenance upon you, and give you peace.

~ *Numbers 6:24-26*

Responding to Christ

Responding to Christ

I come before you, my God, in all of my weakness seeking your strength. Though I am far from the model you set before my eyes, one day I will see you—and upon that seeing, I will become like you. O glorious anticipation! Amen.

~ *Norman Shawchuck, twentieth century*

Lord Jesus Christ, Son of God,
have mercy on me a sinner!

~ *The Jesus Prayer*

Through confession, forgiveness, and surrender

Lord, I am willing to appear to the world and to all to have lost my life, if only I may have made it good in your sight.

~ *Temple Gairdner, 1873–1928*

This I know, that God is for me.
In God, whose word I praise,
in the Lord, whose word I praise,
in God I trust; I am not afraid.

. . . .

For you have delivered my soul from death.

~ *Psalm 56:9-11, 13*

Have mercy on me, O God,
 according to your steadfast love;
according to your abundant
 mercy blot out my transgressions.
Wash me thoroughly from my iniquity,
 and cleanse me from my sin.
For I know my transgressions,
 and my sin is ever before me.
Against you, you alone, have I sinned,
 and done what is evil in your sight,
so that you are justified
   in your sentence
   and blameless when you pass
   judgment.

~ Psalm 51:1-4

Through confession, forgiveness, and surrender

O Lord, deliver me from the torment of doublemindedness. Let me be consistent.

I know you created me with right thinking. But this pain of doublemindedness has plagued me from birth. Where did I get it? . . .

O God, deliver me from this burden of doublemindedness. You are the One who says, "Come!" and then you tell me, "Go!" You have told me, "Be rich." Then you say, "Be poor!" Lord, make up your mind. Surely you must understand doublemindedness. Lord, you must understand me. I am like a wave on the sea, tossed to and fro!

~ *Jim Clardy, twentieth century*

Responding to Christ

Forgive me, most gracious Lord and Father, if this day I have done or said anything to increase the pain of the world. Pardon the unkind word, the impatient gesture, the hard and selfish deed, the failure to show sympathy and kindly help where I have had the opportunity but missed it; and enable me so to live that I may daily do something to lessen the tide of human sorrow, and to add to the sum of human happiness; through him who died for us and rose again, your Son, our Saviour, Jesus Christ. Amen.

~ *A Pocket Prayer Book*

Through confession, forgiveness, and surrender

Father in heaven! Hold not our sins up against us but hold us up against our sins, so that the thought of you when it wakens in our soul, and each time it wakens, should not remind us of what we have committed but of what you did forgive, not of how we went astray but of how you saved us!

~ *Søren Kierkegaard, 1813–1855*

Responding to Christ

I do not understand my own actions. For I do not do what I want, but I do the very things I hate.... Wretched [one] that I am! Who will rescue me from this body of death? Thanks be to God through Jesus Christ our Lord!

~ *Romans 7:15, 24-25*

I bind to me our Lord who stayed
By her whose sin deserved the stone,
Till each accuser turned away;
"Nor do I condemn, you leave atoned."

~ *Gerrit Scott Dawson, twentieth century*

Through confession, forgiveness, and surrender

God, I believe that you have come to me in a very special way through the one we call Jesus. Every day of my life I am astounded that you cared and dared to be present with me in the person of Jesus. Some days I am utterly sure of his presence; other days I am not so sure.

Allow me, in the presence of continuing research and speculation to accept your incarnation in Jesus and receive him as Brother, Companion, Liberator, and Savior. Amen.

~ *Gilbert A. Caldwell, twentieth century*

Responding to Christ

Lord Jesus Christ, I come to you yearning for a new beginning. Reveal yourself to me in this hour; restore and renew my life and bind me once again to yourself. Amen.

~ *Norman Shawchuck, twentieth century*

When my day is too busy and the voices are all too loud, be my good shepherd and my friend. Through fire and water let me be blessed that I may be your living benediction in the world. Amen.

~ *George L. Miller, twentieth century*

Through confession, forgiveness, and surrender

Take, Lord, all my liberty, my memory, my understanding, and my whole will.

You have given me all that I have, all that I am, and I surrender all to your divine will, that you dispose of me.

Give me only your love and your grace. With this I am rich enough, and I have no more to ask.

~ *Ignatius of Loyola, 1491–1556*

This I know, that God is for me.
In God, whose word I praise,
in the Lord, whose word I praise,
in God I trust; I am not afraid.
What can a mere mortal do to me?
My vows to you I must perform,
   O God;
I will render thank offerings to you.
For you have delivered my soul from
   death, and my feet from falling,
so that I may walk before God in the
   light of life.

~ Psalm 56:9-13

Through confession, forgiveness, and surrender

I bind unto myself today
The strong name of the Trinity,
By invocation of the same,
The Three in One and One in Three.
I bind this day to me for ever,
By power of faith, Christ's Incarnation;
His baptism in the Jordan River;
His death on cross for my salvation;
His bursting from the spicèd tomb;
His riding up the heavenly way;
His coming at the day of doom;
I bind unto myself today.

~ *Patrick of Ireland, fifth century*

To you, O God, Father, Son, and Holy Ghost, Creator, Redeemer, and Sanctifier, I give myself up entirely; may I no longer serve myself, but you, all the days of my life.

~ *John Wesley, 1703–1791*

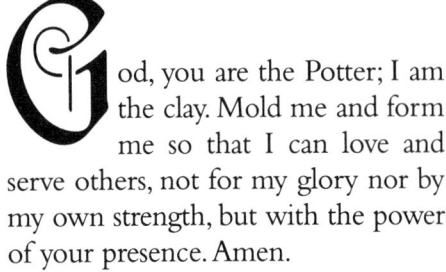

God, you are the Potter; I am the clay. Mold me and form me so that I can love and serve others, not for my glory nor by my own strength, but with the power of your presence. Amen.

~ *Yolanda Pupo-Ortíz, twentieth century*

Through confession, forgiveness, and surrender

I in you, O Lord, I have taken refuge;
   Let me never be put to shame;
  deliver me in your righteousness.
Turn your ear to me,
   come quickly to my rescue;
be my rock of refuge,
   a strong fortress to save me.

~Psalm 31:1-2, NIV

Receive me, O my Saviour, as a sheep that is gone astray but would now return to the great shepherd and bishop of my soul.

~ John Wesley, 1703–1791

Responding to Christ

Lord Jesus Christ, whose cross was raised on Golgotha's brow casting its long shadow over Jerusalem's soul, may the cross be raised at the center of my life, casting its shadow over all my desires and all my motives. In your strong name I pray. Amen.

~ *Norman Shawchuck, twentieth century*

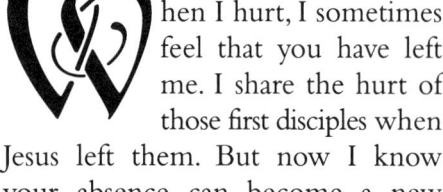

When I hurt, I sometimes feel that you have left me. I share the hurt of those first disciples when Jesus left them. But now I know your absence can become a new space for your presence. Amen.

~ *Richard L. Morgan, twentieth century*

Through suffering and healing

O God, teach us to know that failure is as much a part of life as success—and whether it shall be evil or good depends upon the way we meet it—if we face it listlessly and daunted, angrily or vengefully, then indeed is it evil for it spells death. But if we let our failures stand as guideposts and as warnings—as beacons and as guardians—then is honest failure far better than stolen success, and but a part of that great training which God gives us to make us women and men. The race is not to the swift—nor the battle to the strong, O God. Amen.

~ *W. E. B. Du Bois, twentieth century*

O God, who understandest our distress before we cry unto Thee, lend us Thy strength. In what we sought to do we have failed. Darkness surrounds us, and we see no light save that which shines from Thee.

We know, O Lord, that no night can hide Thee, for the darkness and the light are both alike to Thee. Shed Thy light upon us, that we may see to go forward.

Grant us wisdom to judge aright the present issue and to look steadily toward the future. Help us to put away vain remorse for past mistakes and choose with clearer sight the next step. As we make new plans, may our concern be only to see and to do Thy will.

Through suffering and healing

Give us courage to accept with an unconquered soul whatever may confront us. In outward defeat, help us to remember that nothing save inner surrender can defeat us. Make us brave to face in dignity and strength unwelcome events and the adverse judgment of [others].

O God, as Thou dost labor with [us] to bring in Thy Kingdom, Thou too must suffer as Thy plans are thwarted. But Thou dost ever press forward. Help us to share Thy victory. We pray in the name of our Lord in whom defeat upon His cross was triumph. Amen.

~ *Georgia Harkness, 1891–1974*

Responding to Christ

My Father, if it is possible, may this cup be taken from me. Yet not as I will, but as you will.

~ *Matthew 26:39, NIV*

Keep watch, dear Lord, with those who work, or watch, or weep this night, and give your angels charge over those who sleep. Tend the sick, Lord Christ; give rest to the weary, bless the dying, soothe the suffering, pity the afflicted, shield the joyous; and all for your love's sake. Amen.

~ *The Book of Common Prayer*

Through suffering and healing

Jesus, merciful and faithful priest, out of the quietness of my loneliness, I cry to you: "Have mercy on me." Show me that love which sustains weakness, enlightens darkness and reconciles brokenness and alienation. Let me feel your presence even in the midst of my chaos. When my enemies seem victorious, may I stand firmly assured that you reign supreme. Patient Spirit, as you wait for your children's love, so may I discern your compassion and sense your saying, "Do not be afraid; it is I." Amen.

~ *René O. Bideaux, twentieth century*

Lord, I pray not for tranquillity, nor that my tribulations may cease; I pray for your spirit and your love, that thou grant [me] strength and grace to overcome adversity; through Jesus Christ. Amen.

~ *Girolamo Savonarola, fifteenth century*

Praise be to the God and Father of our Lord Jesus Christ, the Father of compassion and the God of all comfort, who comforts us in all our troubles.

~ *2 Corinthians 1:3-4, NIV*

Through suffering and healing

Remind me anew, O Healer Divine, that pain and sickness, failure and stress are not your punishments. Help me stand on the strong assurance that no matter how dark the valleys in life, each provides me opportunity to grow and draw closer to you.

~ *René O. Bideaux, twentieth century*

Responding to Christ

Blessed Jesus, you did not turn from Martha or Mary when they pled their complaints before you. You bore the accusation of your absence with understanding and compassion.

So do not, I pray, reject me for these faithful cries of anguish. This life is hard! You assured Martha that dead Lazarus would live and told her of the need to trust. So comfort me again in my broken heart that you are the Resurrection and the life. Exhort me to believe beyond what I can see.

When you saw Mary's grief and the tomb, you wept, though you knew you would soon raise him. Oh, weep with me now for all this loss. Though all shall be well, it is not yet, not yet!

Tune your heart to mine and mine to yours that I may know I am not alone when I look upon this torn and tattered world and rail that nothing fits; it is not right.

Catch me up in your passion by the tomb that I may see my rage and sorrow as but little squalls in the storm of your love for the world.

~ *Gerrit Scott Dawson, twentieth century*

Responding to Christ

Almighty God, in this hour, grant me grace that amidst the changes, miseries, or pleasures of life I may keep my mind fixed upon you and improve in grace every day till I am received into your kingdom of eternal happiness. Amen.

~ *Norman Shawchuck, twentieth century*

Through suffering and healing

Most high and glorious God, lighten the darkness of my heart and give me sound faith, firm hope and perfect love. Let me, Lord, have the right feelings and knowledge, properly to carry out the task you have given me.

~ *Francis of Assisi, 1181–1226*

God of new creating,
who beckons us
to the dance of birthing
and sustains us
in our laboring,
hear this prayer:

From fear of the unknown
deliver me.
From doubts of my creativity
deliver me.
From ridicule by those around me
deliver me.
From my excuses about my abilities,
my age, my education,
my looks, my status
deliver me.
With your promise of companionship
comfort me.
With your creative spirit
bless me.

Through suffering and healing

With your pledge of sustenance
strengthen me.
With your embrace of all of me
heal me and set me to motion.
You who called me to life
that you may be born again in me,
blessed be in this and all seasons!

~ *Jan L. Richardson, twentieth century*

e merciful to me, O God,
be merciful to me,
for in you my soul takes
refuge;
in the shadow of your wings I will
take refuge,
until the destroying storms pass by.

~ *Psalm 57:1*

Responding to Christ

Loving God, you have always been our help.

We cry to you and you hear us. You bring healing to your people and deliver us from death. Our grief you have turned to dancing and our sorrow to joy.

Our hearts sing to you, gracious God; we will praise you for ever. Amen.

~ Richard Eslinger, twentieth century

Through suffering and healing

O Lord, when I am unable to help myself, grant me the grace you gave to Lazarus. Bid others brave the smell and open the tomb. Call me by name to life. Bid others unbind me head to toe and see the new creation you have given me.

Gracious Jesus, you are the Resurrection and the life. Teach me to live again.

~ *Gerrit Scott Dawson, twentieth century*

I will extol you, O Lord,
for you have drawn me up,
and did not let my foes
rejoice over me.
O Lord my God, I cried to you for help,
and you have healed me.
O Lord, you brought up my soul from Sheol,
restored me to life from among those gone down to the Pit.

Sing praises to the Lord, O you his faithful ones,
and give thanks to his holy name.
For his anger is but for a moment;
his favor is for a lifetime.
Weeping may linger for the night,
but joy comes with the morning.

~ Psalm 30:1-5

Through suffering and healing

I remember
who I am
in the light of
whose I am.
I give thanks
for the holy places
where you
have revealed
yourself to me,
O God....
And for all the
holy places
I have yet to
know—
This I *do* know:
I will find you. You are
already there—waiting for
me. And I remember who
I am in the light of
whose I am.

~ *Connie Nelson, twentieth century*

Responding to Christ

Oh Lord, where can I meet you? At what point am I broken? From what enemy do I need protection?

God, help me stop lying to myself. In my ignorance and stubbornness I think all is well; I am whole.

All-knowing God, peel off the layers which hide your image in me. Uncover my secrets so I can be completely honest with myself and with You. Help me admit how imperfect I am. Humble me as I face my imperfections.

Ever-present Father, go with me in this struggle. Hold me close as I travel this difficult path. Catch my tears; save them for a holy purpose.

Thank you, Holy One, for hearing me. Be there and celebrate with me as the beautiful creation I am emerges.

~ P. J. Ellis, twentieth century

Yea, though I walk through the valley of the shadow of death, I will fear no evil: for thou art with me; thy rod and thy staff they comfort me.

Thou preparest a table before me in the presence of mine enemies: thou anointest my head with oil; my cup runneth over.

~ Psalm 23:4-5, KJV

Responding to Christ

Almighty God, father of our Lord Jesus Christ, I commit all my ways unto you. I pledge my life to your service. Speak to me of duty and faithfulness. Show me my noble task, and strengthen me to walk in it. Amen.

~ *Norman Shawchuck, twentieth century*

Through daily life and witnessing

Give perfection to beginners, O Father; give intelligence to the little ones; give aid to those who are running their course. Give sorrow to the negligent; give fervour of spirit to the lukewarm. Give to the perfect a good consummation; for the sake of Christ Jesus our Lord. Amen.

~ *Irenaeus, second century*

The things, good Lord, that we pray for, give us the grace to labour for.

~*Thomas More, 1478–1535*

Responding to Christ

Father God, I marvel at the faith of my daughter. There seem to be no gray areas in her life when it comes to trust in you. This experience has taught me something about faith.

Help me understand the difference between faith and knowledge, information and skill. Time and time again I find myself relying only on knowledge, my skill, or the information I possess, instead of my faith.

Help me become like a child, and see the caterpillars among all the leaves of the forest, or hope for the rainbow at the end of the storm, and love the funny little man at the end of the block.

Help me to put my hand in yours, walk with you in the face of cares, and carry you in the midst of need and hurt.

Help me recapture the mystery of my daughter's faith, for to such faith belong the keys to the kingdom of heaven. Make me, like a child, dwell in your kingdom. Amen.

~ *Robert Wood, twentieth century*

O Lord, all my longing is known to you;
my sighing is not hidden from you.

. . . .

Do not forsake me, O Lord;

O my God, do not be far from me; make haste to help me,

O Lord, my salvation.

~ *Psalm 38:9, 21-22*

O God, make the door of this house wide enough to receive all who need human love and fellowship, narrow enough to shut out all envy, pride and strife. Make its threshold smooth enough to be no stumbling-block to children, nor to straying feet, but rugged and strong enough to turn back the tempter's power. God, make the door of this house that gateway to Thine eternal kingdom.

~ *On the door of St. Stephen's in London*

Through daily life and witnessing

Our Father, we thank thee for the food of our body, and for the human love which is the food of our hearts. Bless our family circle, and make this meal a sacrament of love to all who are gathered at this table. But bless thou too that great family of humanity of which we are but a little part. Give to all thy children their daily bread, and let our family not enjoy its comforts in selfish isolation.

~ *Walter Rauschenbusch, 1861–1918*

Responding to Christ

In your compassion you hear the cry of the poor, the needy, and the lonely ones, gracious God. May we also hear the cries of our brothers and sisters, responding in love as you have shown us in your Son, our Savior, Jesus Christ.

~ *Elise S. Eslinger, twentieth century*

Living Christ, I give this situation, this room, all of us here, to you. Take over all the way. Fill this room with your power. Cover us with your light. Take us fully into your hands and heart. Transform us!

~ *Flora Slosson Wuellner, twentieth century*

Through daily life and witnessing

I thank you, O Lord, for the mercies of life, for hard work and relaxation.

May I happily embrace every time given. Renew my spirit, O Lord, in my times of fun, in recreation, in my time off.

All life is your gift: families and friends, the rhythms of life, pleasure, beauty, and the chance to enjoy them.

You are sovereign, O Lord. May every moment of my life be subject to your reign. Refresh me with your Holy Spirit. In Jesus' name. Amen.

~ Thomas A. Langford, twentieth century

Responding to Christ

Deliver me, O God, from too intense an application to even necessary business. I know how this dissipates my thoughts from the one end of all my business, and impairs that lively perception I would ever retain of you standing at my right hand. I know the narrowness of my heart, and that an eager attention to earthly things leaves it no room for the things of heaven. O teach me to go through all my employments with so truly disengaged a heart, that I may still see you in all things, and see you therein as continually looking upon me, and searching my reins; and that I may never impair that liberty of spirit which is necessary for the love of you.

~ *John Wesley, 1703–1791*

Through daily life and witnessing

Dear Lord, break to me this day the "bread of life." My heart is hungry. Save me from thinking, even for a moment, that I can feed my soul on things. Save me from the vain delusion that the piling up of wealth or comforts can satisfy. Help me remember that the real quest for happiness is within. Oh, grant me the radiance of your transforming presence all this day. Amen.

~ Ralph Spaulding Cushman, 1879–1960

Creator God, may there be moments in the routine of this day where your presence is especially known to your child. Fill the hours of my day with meaningful work for your realm. Spare me the mistakes of yesterday and remind me of your grace for the sins of today and tomorrow. As the sun sets on this day, may I continue to celebrate your goodness and rejoice in your love, which knows no limits. In the name of the one who has redeemed me on your behalf. Amen.

~ *Charles Wesley Jordan, twentieth century*

Through daily life and witnessing

Almighty God, we entrust all who are dear to us to Thy never-failing care and love, for this life and the life to come; knowing that Thou art doing for them better things than we can desire or pray for.

~ *The Book of Common Prayer*

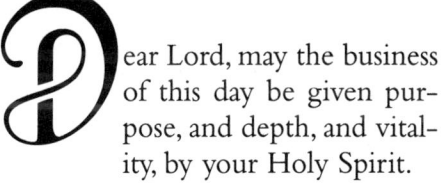

Dear Lord, may the business of this day be given purpose, and depth, and vitality, by your Holy Spirit.

~ *Thomas A. Langford, twentieth century*

Responding to Christ

Teach us, good Lord,
to serve you as you deserve;
to give and not to count the cost;
to fight and not to heed the wounds;
to toil and not to seek for rest;
to labor and not to ask for any reward,
except that of knowing that we do your will;
through Jesus Christ our Lord. Amen.

~ Ignatius of Loyola, 1491–1556

Through daily life and witnessing

May the God who makes all things new, strengthen you to know and claim who you are. May you journey without fear or shame, clearing a path for many and preparing a table for the feast.

~ *Jan L. Richardson, twentieth century*

Ripening in the Spirit

Ever-loving God, who having loved us loves us still, help us to hear again your word, "By this shall they know you are my disciples; that you love one another." Turn our hostility into hospitality and our callousness into care. Through Christ, we pray. Amen.

~ *Norman Shawchuck, twentieth century*

Your word is a lamp to my feet and a light to my path.

~ *Psalm 119:105*

Through the Word and prayer

Come, divine Interpreter, bring me eyes thy book to read, ears the mystic words to hear, words which did from thee proceed, words that endless bliss impart, kept in an obedient heart. Amen.

~ *Charles Wesley, 1707–1762*

Protect us, we beseech you, and all our friends everywhere this night, and awaken in the morning those good thoughts in our hearts, that the words of our Saviour may abide in us and we in him, who has taught us when we pray to say: *Our Father…*

~ *John Wesley, 1703–1791*

O Lamb of God, have mercy upon me. I approach you unworthily, yet am compelled by your Spirit to offer prayers of praise and gratitude for your many blessings. Lord Jesus, prepare me to enter my sacred space where I can be alone with you. You are awaiting me, praying in me and listening to me. Not as I will, but as you know me and my needs, your will be done. I know that my prayers are being answered, even before I offer them. Sustain a meek and humble heart within me, as I offer my prayers to "the One who comes in the name of the Lord."

~ *René O. Bideaux, twentieth century*

Through the Word and prayer

Blessed Lord, you have caused all Holy Scriptures to be written for our learning. Grant us so to hear them, read, mark, learn, and inwardly digest them, that we may embrace and ever hold fast the blessed hope of everlasting life. You have given us this Word in our Savior Jesus Christ, who lives and reigns with you and the Holy Spirit, One God, forever and ever. Amen.

~ *Jim Warren, twentieth century*

Ripening in the Spirit

I need to pray...
I will be quiet for a moment.
Perhaps that is as close as I can come to prayer,
   or perhaps in my quietness,
   I will feel a Spirit not my own.
Eternal God, I am still and I am waiting.
Touch me
   where raw places of anger and
      hurt are to be found.
Heal me
   where open wounds of
      disappointment and pain gape.
Restore me
   where I need restoration.
And reconcile me
   where I am separated from you
      and from others.
How great you are, O God.

You can draw beauty out of
    barrenness,
  courage out of fear,
  and love out of loneliness.
You can make darkness as light
  and silence into singing.
You can help me handle my troubles
  or learn to live with them
    when they cannot be handled.
You can make each day a miracle of
  grace
and fill each night with music.

. . . .

You keep pressing in upon me with
  your forgiveness
    and offering me new chances.
Give me the courage
  to accept the chances that are
  mine this day.

~ *Kenneth G. Phifer, twentieth century*

Listen to my prayer Lord.
Hear the sound of my cry.
Fix your eyes upon me.
Hear the words of my prayer.

Your time has eaten away at my body; it has diminished my strength and taken the sureness from my step.

Time has taken the sharpness of my eyes and has slowed the quickness of my hand. It has barred some of your most precious sounds from my ears.

Time has returned for those things taken, pain and suffering. Slowness and confusion. And I cry to you out of that pain to comfort and support your servant.

I cry out also in hope and thanksgiving, O God, for time has also returned, for those things taken, sure knowledge of your boundless power and love and the forgiveness of my sins.

~ *Dave Senften, twentieth century*

Grant me, O wisdom of God, the courage to expose myself to your Word. Not to manipulate or analyze the scriptures; but, as a patient beneath the surgeon's hand, I entrust my all to your merciful healing and reshaping wisdom. Through your Word, remold me, shape me as your own, Lord Jesus.

~ *René O. Bideaux, twentieth century*

Through the Word and prayer

Make me to remember you on my bed and think upon you when I am waking. You have preserved me from all the dangers of the day past. Under the shadow of your wings let me pass this night in comfort and peace.

~ *John Wesley, 1703–1791*

For these and all Thy gifts of love, we give Thee thanks and praise.
Look down, O Father, from above, and bless us all our days. Amen.

~ *A Pocket Prayer Book*

Be present at our table,
Lord, be here and everywhere adored;
Thy creatures bless, and grant that we may feast in Paradise with Thee. Amen.

~ *A Pocket Prayer Book*

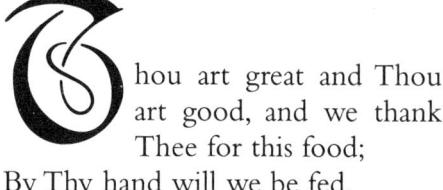

Thou art great and Thou art good, and we thank Thee for this food;
By Thy hand will we be fed,
Give us, Lord, our daily bread. Amen.

~ *A Pocket Prayer Book*

Through the Word and prayer

aster, now you are dismissing your servant in peace,
acccording to your word;
for my eyes have seen your salvation.
Luke 2:29-30

Lord, Jesus, I come to this place with ears tuned to your voice alone. How much I need you, how good to hear you speak my name. Come to me, my Lord, and tell me of your love—even as I long to tell you of my own. Amen.

~ *Norman Shawchuck, twentieth century*

O Lord, why do I worry about tomorrow? Why am I so concerned for the approval of others? Grant me grace to live today with confidence and trust, knowing you reign over every tomorrow.

~ *René O. Bideaux, twentieth century*

Through the love, joy, and peace of God

od, help me to embrace life—
 to perceive beauty
 to confront injustice
 to revere mystery
 to love all.
May my living please you, O God, and my heart find peace and joy in your pleasure. Amen.

~ *Luther E. Smith, Jr., twentieth century*

Gracious God, hear my prayer:
May your mercy make me
more merciful;
your love make me more loving;
your peace make me more peaceful;
and may your power make me more
willing to help the powerless;
your bounty empower me to help
the needy;
and your kindness inspire me to aid
those who suffer.
In Christ's name I pray. Amen.

~ *Jorge A. González, twentieth century*

Through the love, joy, and peace of God

Shine into our hearts, O loving Master, by the pure light of the knowledge of Thyself, and open the eyes of our mind to the contemplation of your teaching, and put into us the fear of your blessed commandments; that trampling down all that is worldly, we may follow a spiritual life, thinking and doing all things according to your good pleasure. For you are our sanctification, and our illumination, and to Thee we render glory, Father, Son, and Holy Spirit, now and ever, and unto ages of ages. Amen.

~ *Eastern Church Liturgy (adapted)*

Grant me, O Lord, to know what is worth knowing, to love what is worth loving, to praise what delights you most,
to value what is precious
 in your sight,
to hate what is offensive to you.
Do not let me judge by what I see,
nor pass sentence according to what
 I hear,
but to judge rightly between things
 that differ,
and above all to search out and to do
 what pleases you,
through Jesus Christ our Lord.

~ Thomas à Kempis, 1380–1471

Through the love, joy, and peace of God

aster of the tools,
sculpt me.
Release from this mass
of stone,
the form you know me to be,
Allow nothing else to shape me,
without your hand.
Flesh out my spirit-form.
Breathe life where there has been
none.
When the work is recognizable,
and I stand, life from stone,
let there be no other ornament
than the thumbprint of God.
Let the toolmarks speak of your
love,
but let my face be yours.
Amen.

~ Ray Buckley, twentieth century

Almighty God,
Teach me timing.
Not the kind used for cars, music, or clocks.
Teach me the kind of timing needed for life in Christ.
Turn, turn, turn.
The world turns in haste. Seldom do I find the time for things of eternal value.
Lord, teach me the seasons, the time for everything under the heavens.
There are times in my life to plant
an idea in the mind of an inquisitive child,
a seed of hope for someone in need,
the gift of trust in one birthing faith.

Through the love, joy, and peace of God

There are times in our lives
  to scatter stones that build walls,
  to gather stones that build bridges
    between alienated individuals.
Teach us the times to seek
  out the fellowship of the body of Christ,
  the solitude of meditation,
  to serve others with humility and love.
For every activity—silence, speech, mourning, dancing, weeping, laughing, tearing, mending, loving, and hating—for all these things we praise you.
Help us use them to know your work in the world and our calling to that work. Amen.

~ Robert Wood, twentieth century

Father, I thank you for the gift of time—for each moment that fills each day. For the promises of tomorrow, I am grateful, but teach me to find joy today. Teach me not only to sense those times when I need to move forward quickly (to plan, to prepare, and to work), but also to sense those times when, in faith, I need to "wait upon the Lord." Give me the grace to just enjoy being your child, to savor the moment and to let tomorrow be concerned for itself.

~ *Jerry Everley, twentieth century*

Through the love, joy, and peace of God

God, grant me the serenity to accept the things I cannot change, the courage to change the things I can, and the wisdom to distinguish the one from the other. Amen.

~ *The Serenity Prayer*

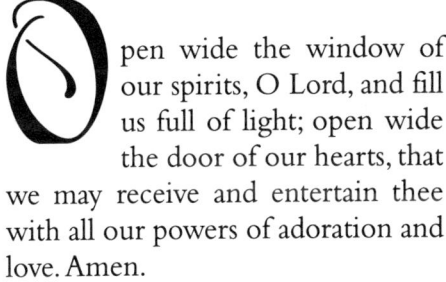

Open wide the window of our spirits, O Lord, and fill us full of light; open wide the door of our hearts, that we may receive and entertain thee with all our powers of adoration and love. Amen.

~ *Christina G. Rossetti, 1830–1894*

Ripening in the Spirit

O God, whose grace and mercy flow like an endless river from your great being, help me now to place myself in the path of your rushing love and limitless compassion, that I may find my spirit renewed. Amen.

~ *Norman Shawchuck, twentieth century*

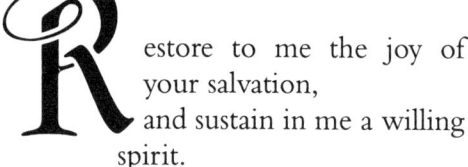

Restore to me the joy of your salvation,
and sustain in me a willing spirit.

~ *Psalm 51:12*

Through the love, joy, and peace of God

Lord, let your soothing, healing, cleansing Spirit wash across our bruised and battered lives. Take away all that festers and spoils within—all envy, discontent, all malice, every jealous thought. And teach us the true meaning of contentment based in love. Reveal to us the way to peace, that peace that passes understanding. Amen.

~ *J. Barrie Shepherd, twentieth century*

Blessed are you, O Lord, who has nourished me from my youth up, who gives food to all flesh. Fill our hearts with joy and gladness, that we, always having all sufficiency in all things, may abound to every good work in Christ Jesus our Lord, through whom to you be glory, honour, might, majesty, and dominion, forever and ever. Amen.

~ *The Clementine Liturgy, first century (adapted)*

Through the love, joy, and peace of God

Give me, O Lord, a steadfast heart,
which no unworthy affection may drag downwards;
give me an unconquered heart,
which no tribulation can wear out;
give me an upright heart,
which no unworthy purpose may tempt aside.
Bestow on me also, O Lord my God,
understanding to know you,
diligence to seek you,
wisdom to find you,
and a faithfulness that may finally embrace you,
through Jesus Christ our Lord, Amen.

~ *Thomas Aquinas, 1225–1274*

Your streaks at sunset whisper to me, Lord—whisper of your peace.

In this holy Garden, you quiet my soul, still my busy body, comfort my yearning heart....

Your tree, Holy Lord, centers me in seasons of despair. With reaching branches, kissed by your sunlight, cooled by your stars, she embraces your being.

You are here, Lord...
 calling me to prayer.
You are here, Lord...
 listening to my tears.
You are here, Lord...
 waiting patiently for me.
You are here, Lord...
 You are here. Amen and amen.

~ *Colleen McGloughlin, twentieth century*

Through the love, joy, and peace of God

O Giver of every good and perfect gift, if at any time it pleases you to work by my hand, teach me to discern what is my own from what is another's and to render unto you the things that are yours. As all the good that is done on earth, you do yourself, let me ever return to you all the glory. Let me as a pure crystal transmit all the light you pour upon me.

~ *John Wesley, 1703–1791*

Our Lord Jesus, whose word is always authority, speak to me now, that I may hear your special word for me today.

~ *Norman Shawchuck, twentieth century*

O God our Father, we rejoice that nothing can separate us from Thy love and care. Thou art our light in darkness, our strength in adversity, our hope when all else fails. Cleanse us… and give us power to put away all hurtful things. Make strong our souls; enlarge our compassion; help us to love all…even our enemies. In Christ's name. Amen.

~ *Georgia Harkness, 1891–1974*

Through truth, discernment, and perseverance

O God, teach me the secret of happiness, and enable me to express my love for you in nobility of character and unselfish conduct. There is no delight so deep and so true as the joy of doing your will. There is no blessedness like that of communing with you. Give me, I pray you, a clearer perception of your will, and harmonize my daily walk with your purposes. In Christ's blessed name I pray. Amen.

~ *Grover Carlton Emmons, 1886–1944*

God of community,
who calls us to be in relationship
with one another
and who has promised to dwell
wherever two or three are gathered,
hear this prayer:
By your Spirit you have graced each
of us with differing gifts.
To one you have given the speaking
of wisdom,
to another, the utterance of knowledge,
to another, faith,
to another, gifts of healing,
to another, the working of miracles,
to another, prophecy,
to another, discernment of spirits,
to another, various kinds of tongues,
and to another, the interpretation of
tongues. (1 Cor. 12:7-10)

Through truth, discernment, and perseverance

For these and all gifts by which you bless our communities, I give you thanks.
And for any way in which I have shared in deepening the wounds of the body of Christ,
I seek your love-filled forgiveness.
Open my eyes, O God, to perceive the gifts you have placed within me and to honor the differing gifts which my sisters and brothers offer.
Bless our hands, our hearts, our vision to work together....
By these acts may we bring healing to the tender, wounded, and strong body of Christ,
rising in our midst.

~ *Jan L. Richardson, twentieth century*

Christ, my Servant Lord, I seek to do your will yet I am so often discouraged by what I see and what I know. What I experience often beats me down, driving out my joy and dreams and even the sight of you. But your faithful Spirit dwells with me, stirring my heart and my mind. And so I pray that you who are the Dreamer, the Joy and the Hope of the Ages, would sow in me dreams and visions of what is yet to be, that what is may never so fill my seeing that I am unable to see you, so conquer my knowing that I cease to know you, or so paralyze my doing that I fail to serve you. Amen.

~ *Minerva G. Carcaño, twentieth century*

Through truth, discernment, and perseverance

Deliver me, O God, from all idolatrous love of any creature. Preserve me from all such blind affection. Be a guard to all my desires. And be my security, that I may never open my heart to anything but out of love to you.

~ John Wesley, 1703–1791

My Lord and friend, in the quietness of this hour, reconcile my contrary motives and conflicting desires. Give me a singleness of purpose that I may come into your presence unashamed and sit under your gaze without blushing. Amen.

~ *Norman Shawchuck, twentieth century*

If now I have found favor in your sight, O Lord, I pray, let the Lord go with us. Although this is a stiff-necked people, pardon our iniquity and our sin, and take us for your inheritance.

~ *Exodus 34:9*

Through reconciliation, justice, and unity in Christ

Today is a gift, O Lord, a gift of grace from you.

Release in me your wondrous power and set me free. For I am chained by doubt and guilt and need your healing touch.

You have proclaimed release for the captives, the down-trodden, the oppressed. And now I pray that you will find a way to release me from those private sins and public deeds that weigh me down and hold me back from being all that you meant me to be. Amen.

~ *Ron Patterson, twentieth century*

O God of the lonely,
Remember this day those who need the warmth of human touch, the sound of loving voice, the presence of caring spirit. The lonely are all around us.... Cause your Spirit of Loving Concern to touch some man and woman, some boy and girl, so that each will be moved to reach out to one alone who awaits

    a telephone call
    a note
    a visit
    a hug or kiss
    a firm handshake
    a warm meal
    a long walk
    a caring letter.

O God of the Lonely
   send those ambassadors of your love
   so that your lonely children
   will be lonely no more.
And may those who are lonely
Ever be open to your abiding presence, that they will know—though lonely—
   They are not alone!
                              Amen.

~ *Woodie W. White, twentieth century*

God of all peoples and all nations, I call for your blessing mindful that you have mothered and fathered all of us. God grant me the vision to welcome you into my midst. Charge me to be your message-carrier. Gather me up even as a mother scoops up her children and hugs them so that I may know courage, learn hope, and speak love.

~ Thom White Wolf Fassett
twentieth century

Through reconciliation, justice, and unity in Christ

Heavenly Father, Thou knowest the weakness and cowardliness of my heart. Thou knowest how much I care for the opinion of [others]. Help me, I beseech Thee, to care more for what will please Thee. Make me strong and courageous that I may never be afraid to do my duty. Give me grace and courage to speak when and as I should. Let me never betray Thee, O Christ, my Lord and Saviour, either by word or act. Amen.

~ Ralph Spaulding Cushman, 1879–1960

I offer up unto you my prayers and intercessions, for those especially who have in any matter hurt, grieved, or found fault with me, or who have done me any damage or displeasure.

For all those also whom, at any time I may have vexed, troubled, burdened, and scandalized, by words or deeds, knowingly or in ignorance; that you would grant us all equally pardon for our offenses against each other.

Take away from our hearts, O Lord, all suspiciousness, indignation, wrath, and contention, and whatsoever may hurt charity, and lessen [filial] love.

Through reconciliation, justice, and unity in Christ

Have mercy, O Lord, have mercy on those that crave your mercy, give grace unto them that stand in need thereof, and make us such as that we may be worthy to enjoy your grace, and go forward to life eternal. Amen.

~ Thomas à Kempis, 1380–1471

Lord, I pray that your justice, tempered by your mercy, may never be a mere abstraction for me. Open my eyes and my heart to seek ways to do justice in my own life and in my community. As I pray and work for justice, help me to extend your love to all I encounter, both those who work with me and those who oppose me. When I am wrong, help me to accept correction graciously. Above all, in all things, enable me to see the face of Christ in every person I meet, and to act accordingly. Amen.

~ *Joanne H. Davis, twentieth century*

Through reconciliation, justice, and unity in Christ

Lord, help me to show toward [others] that kindness which I have so often craved from them. May I think of my neighbor not as my rival who would undo me, but as my brother [or sister] who needs me. Give me the compassion of Jesus that I may never be able to turn coldly from anyone who needs me. Make me quick to hear the cry of the suffering. Turn my feet toward the house of sorrow. May I know the joy of carrying hope to hearts that have long been strangers to hope....Help me to relieve the heart-hunger of the neglected. For Jesus' sake. Amen.

~ *A Pocket Prayer Book*

Almighty God, have mercy on the people of this land. Forgive our hardness of heart and contempt of your commandments.

Help us to lay aside the pride that deludes us, the prejudice that blinds us, and the hatred that destroys us.

Give to our leaders patience and wisdom and the humility to seek your way forward. May your truth guide them, your justice direct them, your love unite them, so that your will may be done through Jesus Christ our Lord.

~ *Cecil Kerr, twentieth century*

Through reconciliation, justice, and unity in Christ

Lord, make me an instrument of your peace.
Where there is hatred, let me sow love.
Where there is injury, pardon;
Where there is doubt, faith;
Where there is despair, hope;
Where there is darkness, light;
Where there is sadness, joy.
O divine Master, grant that I may not so much seek
To be consoled, as to console,
To be understood, as to understand,
To be loved, as to love,
For it is in giving that we receive;
It is in pardoning that we are pardoned;
It is in dying that we are born to eternal life.

~ *Anonymous*

Our Lord, before your trials of suffering you prayed that all your disciples might be one in Spirit. Grant that we may be bound together in love for one another and in obedience to you, that the world may see and believe. In Jesus, our Lord. Amen.

~ *Norman Shawchuck, twentieth century*

Jesus, our mentor of wholeness, guide me through the streets of my journey. Open my eyes and my ears to the guiding of God's spirit who calls me to costly faithfulness and to joyous wholeness.

~ *Beth A. Richardson, twentieth century*

Through reconciliation, justice, and unity in Christ

My Lord Jesus Christ,
two graces I beg of you
before I die:
the first is that in my lifetime
I may feel, in my soul and in my body, as far as possible,
that sorrow which you, sweet Jesus, endured in the hour of your most bitter passion;
the second is that I may feel in my heart, as far as possible,
that abundance of love with which you, Son of God,
were inflamed, so as willingly to endure so great a passion for us sinners.

~ *Francis of Assisi, 1181–1226*

I pray that, according to the riches of his glory, he may grant that you may be strengthened in your inner being with power through his Spirit, and that Christ may dwell in your hearts through faith, as you are being rooted and grounded in love. I pray that you may have the power to comprehend, with all the saints, what is the breadth and length and height and depth, and to know the love of Christ that surpasses knowledge, so that you may be filled with all the fullness of God.

~ Ephesians 3:16-19

Through reconciliation, justice, and unity in Christ

Dearest Lord, teach me to be generous;
Teach me to serve thee as thou deservest;
To give and not to count the cost,
To fight and not to heed the wounds,
To toil and not to seek for rest,
To labour and not to seek reward,
Save that of knowing that I do thy will.

~ *Ignatius of Loyola, 1491–1556*

You are the First and the Last, the Alpha and the Omega; all life begins and ends in you, Lord Jesus. Why, therefore, do I struggle to be in control? Why am I in such a hurry to fill my days with things that have no eternal value? And, moreover, why do I postpone those activities that nurture the promises of eternity? Where is the passion to do your will in all things? O God, I am bold to claim the fullness of your mercy and faithfulness. I pray for the grace to submit all to you, patience to wait upon your timing, hunger for holiness, and discernment of your will. May this

Through reconciliation, justice, and unity in Christ

---

weak and unworthy one stand ever ready to enter the place you have already prepared, O Jesus, my resurrection.

~ *René O. Bideaux, twentieth century*

Help each of us, gracious God, to live in such magnanimity and restraint that the Head of the church may never have cause to say to any one of us, "This is my body, broken by you." Amen.

~ *Chinese Prayer*

Gracious and Creative God of the Church, I pray that you will continue to look with favor and compassion upon that unique and distinctive expression of the church where I attend.

We talk of diminishing membership; we place too much energy and expectation in restructuring; at times we fail to be bold and courageous.

Yet God you have used us, sometimes in spite of ourselves. May I, may we, begin to come close to being the Church that you expect us to be and want us to be. Amen.

~ Gilbert A. Caldwell, twentieth century

Through reconciliation, justice, and unity in Christ

Dear Jesus, Prince of Peace, I am disturbed by the existence of so much violence in our world, which is tearing nations apart and damaging the lives of our youth. I pray that you will touch my heart with the urgency of your message of love and that you will enable me to become an effective ambassador of your peace. Give me the courage, the will, and the wisdom I need to neutralize the causes of violence. Help me find ways to counteract the glorification of violence with the message that the way of Christ is the way of peace.
~ *Ray and Delaine DeHainaut*
twentieth century

Great Shepherd of souls, bring home into your fold all that are gone astray. Preserve your Church from all heresy and schism, from all that persecute or oppose the truth; and give your ministers wisdom and holiness and the powerful aid of your blessed Spirit.

~ John Wesley, 1703–1791

Acknowledgments

Acknowledgments

While every effort has been made to secure permission, we may have failed in a few cases to trace or contact the copyright holder. We apologize for any inadvertent oversight or error.

Scripture quotations not otherwise identified are from the New Revised Standard Version of the Bible, © 1989 by the Division of Christian Education of the National Council of the Churches of Christ in the USA. Used by permission. All rights reserved.

KJV designates quotations from the King James Version of the Bible.

Scripture quotations designated RSV are from the Revised Standard Version of the Bible, copyrighted 1846, 1952, and ©1971 by the Division of Christian Education, National Council of the Churches of Christ in the USA. Used by permission.

Scripture quotations designated NIV are from the *Holy Bible, New International Version*. Copyright © 1973, 1978, 1984 International Bible Society. Used by permission of Zondervan Bible Publishers.

Acknowledgments

An African Prayer (20). From *From Grim to Green Pastures* by Richard L. Morgan. Nashville, TN: Upper Room Books, 1994.

Augustine of Hippo (25). From *The Confessions of St. Augustine*, trans by F. J. Sheed. London: Sheed & Ward, 1944.

Joseph B. Bethea (35). From *The Upper Room Disciplines 1983*. Nashville, TN: The Upper Room, 1982. Used by permission.

René O. Bideaux (61, 63, 94, 100, 104, 142). Prayers used by permission.

The Book of Common Prayer (60, 87). New York: Oxford University Press, 1990.

Ray Buckley (26, 109). Prayers used by permission.

Gilbert A. Caldwell (49, 144). Prayers used by permission.

Minerva G. Carcaño (124). Prayer used by permission.

Edward G. Carroll, Sr. (22). Prayer used by permission.

Chinese Prayer (143). From *The United*

Acknowledgments

Methodist Hymnal. Nashville, TN: The United Methodist Publishing House, 1989.

Clardy, Jim (45). Prayer used by permission.

The Clementine Liturgy (116). From *Famous Prayers.* Nashville, TN: Abingdon Press, 1987.

Ralph Spaulding Cushman (85, 131). From *A Pocket Prayer Book and Devotional Guide.* Nashville, TN: The Upper Room, 1941. Used by permission.

Joanne H. Davis (134). From *The Prayer Calendar 1996.* © General Board of Global Ministries, The United Methodist Church, 475 Riverside Drive, New York, NY 10115. Used by permission.

Gerrit Scott Dawson (28, 48, 64, 71). From *Writing on the Heart.* Nashville, TN: Upper Room Books, 1995. Used by permission.

Ray and Delaine DeHainaut (145). From *The Prayer Calendar 1996.* © General Board of Global Ministries, The United Methodist Church, 475 Riverside Drive, New York, NY 10115. Used by permission.

John Donne (24). From *Eerdmans' Book of*

ACKNOWLEDGMENTS

Famous Prayers. Grand Rapids, MI: William B. Eerdmans Publishing Co., 1984.

W. E. B. Du Bois (57). From *Prayers for Dark People*, by W. E. B. Du Bois, ed. by Herbert Aptheker. Amherst: University of Massachusetts Press, 1980. Copyright © 1980 by The University of Massachusetts Press. Used by permission.

Eastern Church Liturgy (107). From *Prayers of the Christian Church*, ed. by J. Manning Potts. Nashville, TN: The Upper Room, 1980.

P. J. Ellis (74). From *Psalms of Academy #11* (August 1995). The Academy for Spiritual Formation. Used by permission.

Grover Carlton Emmons (121). From *Alone with God*. Nashville, TN: The Upper Room, 1945. Used by permission.

Erin (17). From *Children and Prayer*, by Betty Shannon Cloyd. Nashville, TN: The Upper Room, 1997. Used by permission.

Elise S. Eslinger (19, 82). From *The Upper Room Worshipbook*. Nashville, TN: The Upper Room, 1985. Used by permission.

Acknowledgments

Richard Eslinger (70). From *The Upper Room Worshipbook*. Nashville, TN: The Upper Room, 1985. Used by permission.

Jerry Everley (112). Prayer used by permission.

Thom White Wolf Fassett (130). Prayer used by permission.

Francis of Assisi (14). From *Eerdmans' Book of Famous Prayers*. Grand Rapids, MI: William B. Eerdmans Publishing Co., 1984.

Francis of Assisi (67). From *Saint Francis Prayer Book*. Chicago: Franciscan Herald Press, 1978. Used by permission.

Francis of Assisi (139). From *The United Methodist Hymnal*. Nashville, TN: The United Methodist Publishing House, 1989.

Temple Gairdner (43). From *Eerdmans' Book of Famous Prayers*. Grand Rapids, MI: William B. Eerdmans Publishing Co., 1984.

Jorge A. González (106). Prayer used by permission.

George R. Graham (32). Prayer from *Alive Now*, January/February 1996. Used by permission.

ACKNOWLEDGMENTS

Georgia Harkness (58, 120). From *The Glory of God: Poems and Prayers for Devotional Use*. New York: Abingdon-Cokesbury Press, 1943. Used by permission.

Ignatius of Loyola (51). From *Eerdmans' Book of Famous Prayers*. Grand Rapids, MI: William B. Eerdmans Publishing Co., 1984.

Ignatius of Loyola (141). From *Famous Prayers*. Nashville, TN: Abingdon Press, 1987.

Ignatius of Loyola (88). From *The United Methodist Hymnal*. Nashville, TN: The United Methodist Publishing House, 1989.

Irenaeus (77). From *Famous Prayers*. Nashville, TN: Abingdon Press, 1987.

Charles Wesley Jordan (86). Prayer used by permission.

Cecil Kerr (136). From *The Prayer Calendar 1996.* © General Board of Global Ministries, The United Methodist Church, 475 Riverside Drive, New York, NY 10115. Used by permission.

Søren Kierkegaard (47). From *The Journals of Søren Kierkegaard*, ed. and trans. by

Acknowledgments

Alexander Dru. London: Oxford University Press, 1938. Used by permission.

Thomas A. Langford (38, 83, 87). From *Prayer and the Common Life*. Nashville, TN: The Upper Room, 1984. Used by permission.

Martin Luther (30). From *Eerdmans' Book of Famous Prayers*. Grand Rapids, MI: William B. Eerdmans Publishing Co., 1984.

Colleen McGloughlin (118). From *Psalms of Academy #8* (May 1993). The Academy for Spiritual Formation. Used by permission.

George L. Miller (50). From *Jubilee: Readings through the Year from Alive Now*. Nashville, TN: Upper Room Books, 1996. Used by permission.

Dwight L. Moody (27). From *Eerdmans' Book of Famous Prayers*. Grand Rapids, MI: William B. Eerdmans Publishing Co., 1984.

Thomas More (77). From *Famous Prayers*. Nashville, TN: Abingdon Press, 1987.

Richard L. Morgan (56). From *From Grim to Green Pastures*. Nashville, TN: Upper Room Books, 1994. Used by permission.

ACKNOWLEDGMENTS

Connie Nelson (73). From *Psalms of Academy #8* (May 1993). The Academy for Spiritual Formation. Used by permission.

Patrick of Ireland (53). "St. Patrick's Breastplate" from *Writing on the Heart* by Gerrit Scott Dawson. Nashville, TN: Upper Room Books, 1995.

Ron Patterson (127). Prayer from *Alive Now*, January/February 1996. Used by permission.

Kenneth G. Phifer (36, 96). *A Book of Uncommon Prayer*. Nashville, TN: The Upper Room, 1981. Used by permission.

A Pocket Prayer Book and Devotional Guide, comp. by Ralph Spaulding Cushman (46, 101, 102, 135). Nashville, TN: The Upper Room, 1941.

Yolanda Pupo-Ortíz (54). Prayer used by permission.

Walter Rauschenbusch (16). From *Eerdmans' Book of Famous Prayers*. Grand Rapids, MI: William B. Eerdmans Publishing Co., 1984.

Walter Rauschenbusch (81). From *Prayers of the Social Awakening*. Boston: The Pilgrim Press, 1910.

Acknowledgments

Richard of Chichester (21). From *Eerdmans' Book of Famous Prayers*. Grand Rapids, MI: William B. Eerdmans Publishing Co., 1984.

Beth A. Richardson (138). From *Jubilee: Readings through the Year from Alive Now*. Nashville, TN: Upper Room Books, 1996. Used by permission.

Jan L. Richardson (68, 89, 122). From *Sacred Journeys: A Woman's Book of Daily Prayer*. Nashville, TN: Upper Room Books, 1995. Used by permission.

Christina G. Rossetti (113). From *The United Methodist Hymnal*. Nashville, TN: The United Methodist Publishing House, 1989.

Girolamo Savonarola (62). From *The United Methodist Hymnal*. Nashville, TN: The United Methodist Publishing House, 1989.

Dave Senften (98). From *Psalms of Academy #8* (May 1993). The Academy for Spiritual Formation. Used by permission.

Norman Shawchuck and Rueben P. Job (13, 23, 33, 42, 50, 56, 66, 76, 92, 104, 114, 120, 126, 138). From *A Guide to Prayer for*

Acknowledgments

All God's People. Nashville, TN: Upper Room Books, 1990. Used by permission.

J. Barrie Shepherd (115). From *Aspects of Love*. Nashville, TN: Upper Room Books, 1995. Used by permission.

Luther E. Smith, Jr. (105). Prayer used by permission.

Steve Smith (34). From *Psalms of Academy #11* (August 1995). The Academy of Spiritual Formation. Used by permission.

Thomas à Kempis (108). From *Eerdmans' Book of Famous Prayers*. Grand Rapids, MI: William B. Eerdmans Publishing Co., 1984.

Thomas à Kempis (132). From *Famous Prayers*. Nashville, TN: Abingdon Press, 1987.

Thomas Aquinas (117). From *Eerdmans' Book of Famous Prayers*. Grand Rapids, MI: William B. Eerdmans Publishing Co., 1984.

Traditional Native American Prayer (18): From *The United Methodist Hymnal*. Nashville, TN: The United Methodist Publishing House, 1989.

Jim Warren (95). Prayer used by permission.

Charles Wesley (93). From *The United Methodist Hymnal*. Nashville, TN: The United Methodist Publishing House, 1989.

John Wesley (24, 54, 55, 93, 119, 125, 146). From *John Wesley's Prayers*, ed. by Frederick C. Gill. New York: Abingdon-Cokesbury Press, 1952.

John Wesley (84, 101). From *The Works of John Wesley*, vol. 11. Grand Rapids, MI: Zondervan Publishing House, n.d.

Woodie W. White (128). Prayer used by permission.

Robert Wood (78, 110). From *A Thirty-Day Experiment in Prayer*. Nashville, TN: The Upper Room, 1978.

Flora Slosson Wuellner (82). From *Heart of Healing, Heart of Light*. Nashville, TN: Upper Room Books, 1992. Used by permission.

About the Compiler

René O. Bideaux lives at Lake Junaluska, North Carolina, and is retired. He has served as a local church pastor in the Southern New England and North Carolina Annual Conferences. He has also been a district superintendent, a missionary in Costa Rica, and a staff member at the Hinton Rural Life Center and at the General Board of Global Ministries. René has been active in the Walk to Emmaus and has served on leadership teams for the Academy for Spiritual Formation.